Look Out for Snakes!

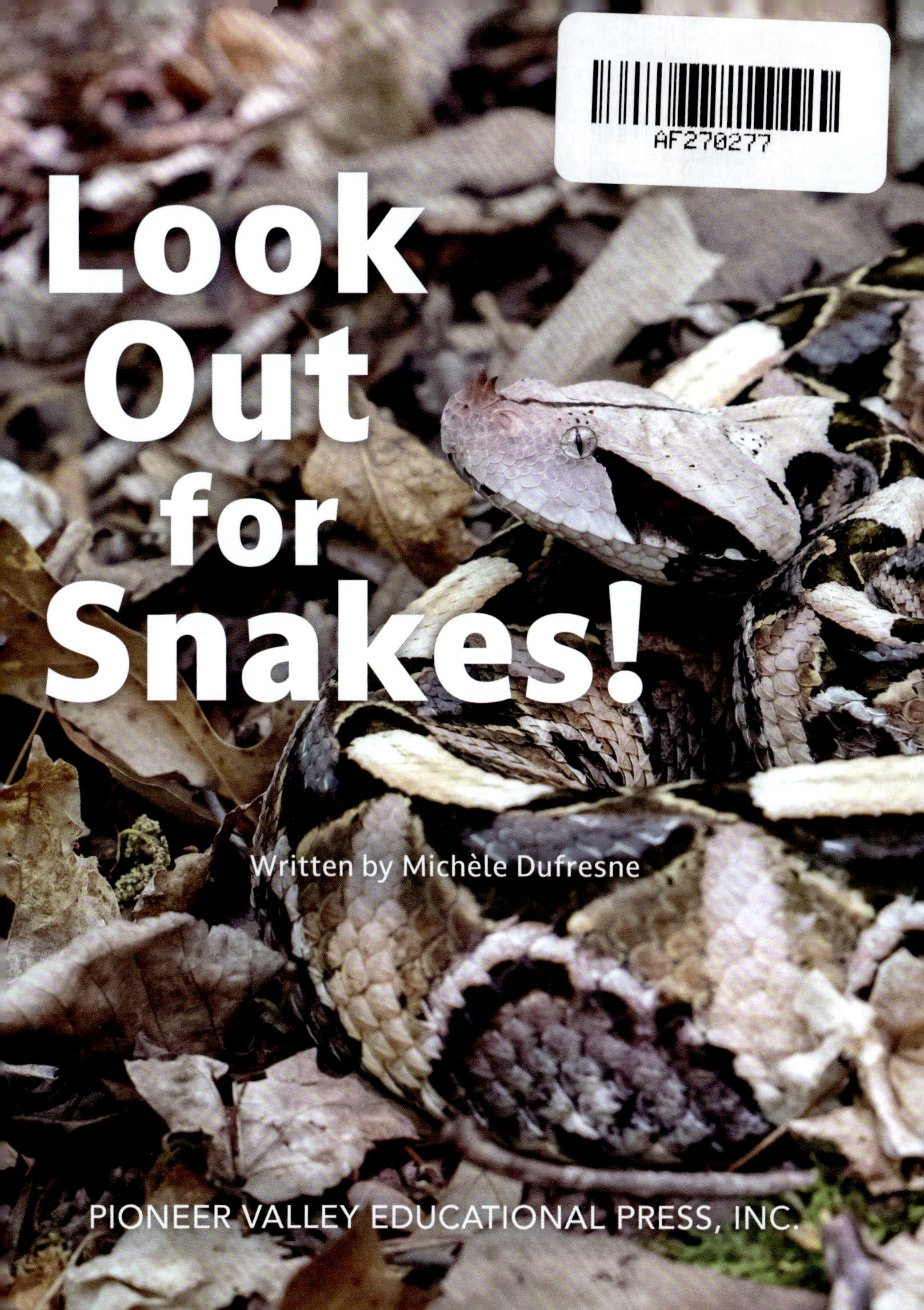

Written by Michèle Dufresne

PIONEER VALLEY EDUCATIONAL PRESS, INC.

Here is a **snake**.

Snakes do not have legs.

The snake went up, up, up the **tree**.

Snakes have bodies that are long and strong. They use their muscles to slither and also to swim and climb.

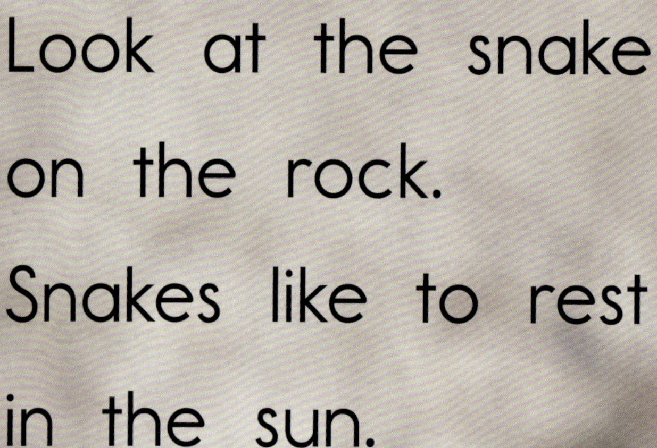

Look at the snake
on the rock.
Snakes like to rest
in the sun.

Snakes are reptiles. Like all reptiles, they are cold-blooded. They sit in the sun to raise their body temperature.

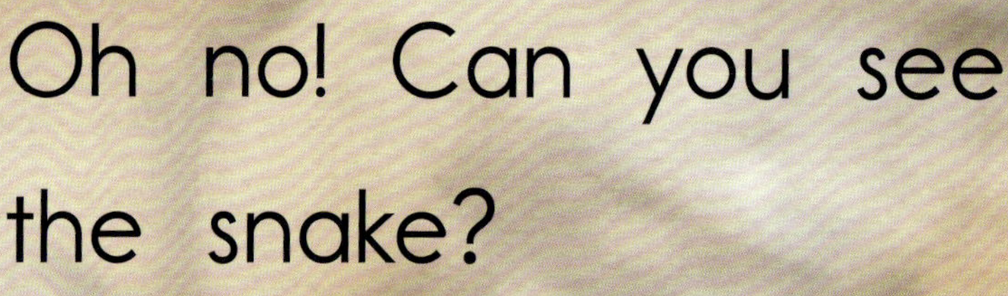

Oh no! Can you see the snake?
Look out where you step!

This is an Arizona black rattlesnake. It can change color to blend in with the ground.

A snake can blend into the **leaves.**

Look at the specks on the snake. The specks help it blend in.

This is a speckled kingsnake. It likes to live in wet places like swamps. To scare away predators, it shakes its tail like a rattlesnake.

Snakes do not have nests. Some snakes spend the **winter** in dens.

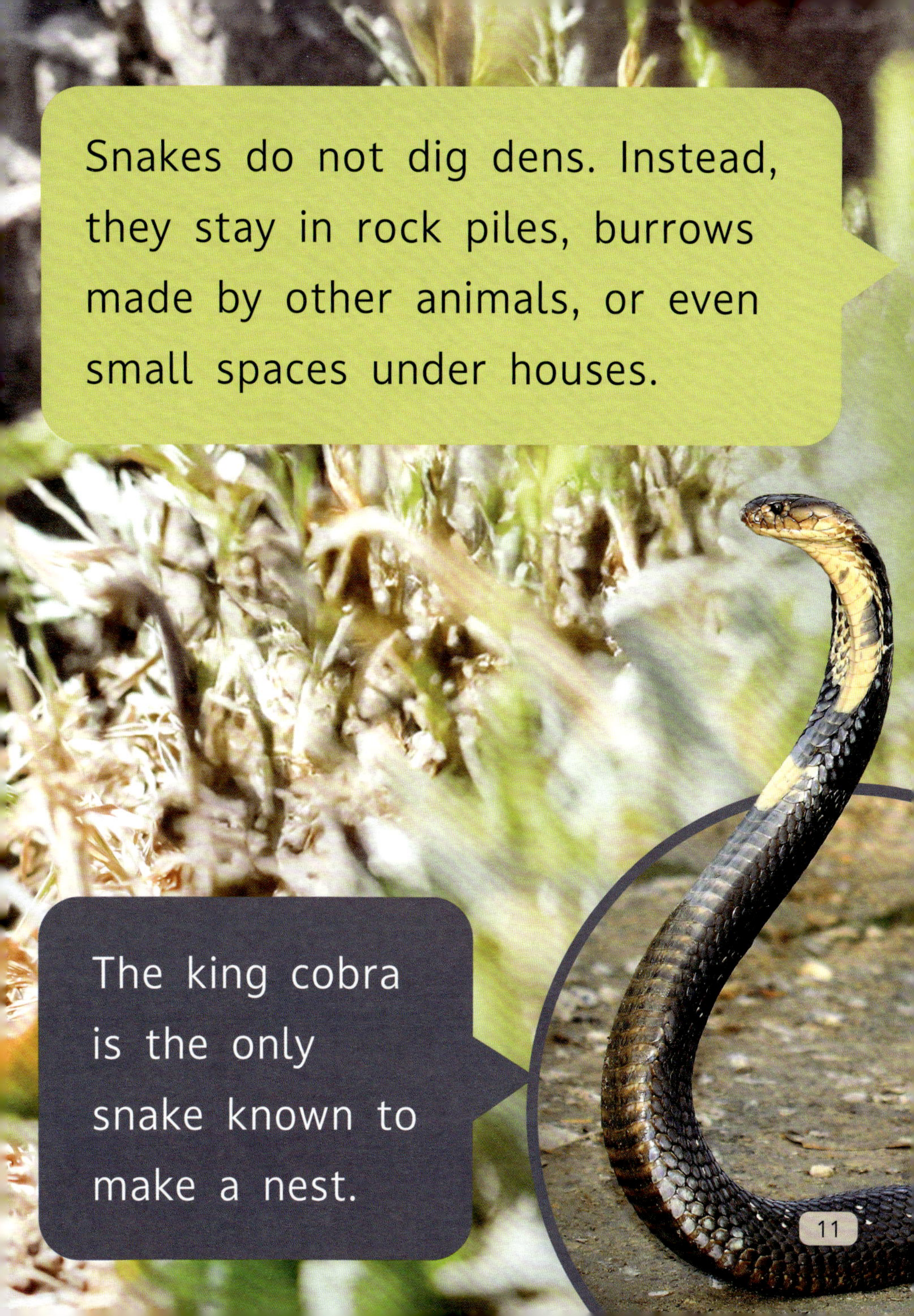

Snakes do not dig dens. Instead, they stay in rock piles, burrows made by other animals, or even small spaces under houses.

The king cobra is the only snake known to make a nest.

glossary

snake

tree

leaves

winter